Contents

Acknowledgments 5

Preface..6

Forward 7

Chapter 1   Struck Down, But Not Destroyed...........8

Chapter 2   To Forgive or Not to Forgive................12

Chapter 3   And A Funeral..14

Chapter 4   Joy and Forgiveness..............................16

Chapter 5   Fairy Tales and Optimism....................20

Chapter 6   Stupid vs. Trusting................................25

Chapter 7   His Hands & A Treasure.......................31

Chapter 8   Hangover, Sympathy & Impatience......35

Chapter 9   Passionate Love & Ohio Questions......38

Chapter 10   Motel 6 & The Holy Spirit....................40

Chapter 11   Salty Tears & Murky Swamps..............42

Chapter 12   A Kiss & A Bandage..............................45

Chapter 13 The Letter...47

Chapter 14 Closing on the House............................51

Chapter 15 Writers Block & Drunk Cowboys..........53

Chapter 16 Where's My Song...................................56

Chapter 17 Little Reminders....................................59

Chapter 18 Kemah & A Wandering Mind...............61

Chapter 19 A Prayer for Healing & Peace...............63

Chapter 20 Anti-Depressants & A Warning Label..65

Chapter 21 Loneliness & Anticipation.....................67

Chapter 22 On My Knees...69

Chapter 23 Setbacks & Jerks....................................72

Chapter 24 Life Lessons...74

Chapter 25 The Anniversary....................................75

Chapter 26 Diary of a Mad White Irish Girl............77

Chapter 27 By The Grace of God.............................79

Epilogue..81

Hell Hath No

The Diary of a Woman Scorned

**Written By
Tara Vincent**

© **2010 by Tara and Kenneth Vincent**

Published in the United States in 2010 by **IMPACT** Publishing, LLC
PO Box 20355, Beaumont, TX 77720-0355

First Printing: May, 2010

ALL RIGHTS RESERVED. No portion of this book may be reproduced, stored in a retrieval system, or transmitted in any form or by any means – for example, electronic, photocopy, recording – without the prior written permission of the publisher.

All scripture references taken from the New International Version except where noted. King James Version noted as KJV.

ISBN: 978-0-9845858-0-9

Acknowledgments

For my husband, whom I love now more than ever before. Thank you for being humble enough to let me print our personal life in order to help maybe only one.

I would also like to thank the Rev. Joseph Granberry, who stuck his neck out for a couple that no one else wanted to take a chance on. Your faith in God, your kindness, and your mentoring encouraged us to take this journey with God. A path I will never regret taking.

A thousand thanks to our family that supported us emotionally, spiritually and even financially until we could get back on our feet. One day, I hope we can bless you as much as you have blessed us.

Finally, a special thank you to BJ and Donna Compton and Restoring the Foundations for being sensitive to the Holy Spirit and blessing us immensely with your ministry. You have given us the tools to not only find complete healing and deliverance, but to walk it out as well.

Preface
by Tara Vincent

I feel it is important that everyone who reads this book understand the raw emotions one feels when faced with a crisis such as this. This "rawness" is reflected in several of my journal entries, and has been left in place to communicate accurately the healing process I went through. It is not my intent to portray ungodly attitudes or actions that are reflected in my entries as somehow godly.

There is an extreme amount of vulnerability in printing my deepest thoughts, unedited. I believe God wants me to be transparent and honest. The testimony I have, I feel needs to be shared. I have found hope and healing. It is my prayer that women in all phases of relationships: premarital, married or divorced, can glean hope and healing in their own personal lives.

Forward
by Kenneth Vincent

Words can't express the sorrow and shame I felt when I was confronted with my adulterous behavior, and brought to a place where I had to confess my sin to my wife. The feelings of shame and sorrow were only worsened by the fact that I was a minister of the Gospel. I had pledged myself to be above reproach. I had failed my God, my wife, my family, and myself.

When I confessed my infidelity, I was not sure if Tara would stay with me. There were many reasons (not excuses) for the choices I made. But there were no guarantees that Tara would choose to stay in our marriage. She had every right to leave. But what makes her so much like Christ, is what took her on this journey you are about to read. It is Tara's ability to give grace and unmerited forgiveness to those who don't deserve it, namely me.

It is my hope that you find this record of Tara's journey into depths of pain, suffering, healing and rejoicing both inspirational and thought-provoking regarding your relationships.

It has been my experience that there is always hope. I hope you find it here and in the arms of your loving God.

1

Struck Down, But Not Destroyed

May 14

Today is Friday. I found out on Sunday. Sunday was May 9th, 2004. Sunday was also Mother's Day and it was also my baby's three-month birthday. Sunday was also one of, if not THE, worst days of my entire life. There really are no words to describe the pain and rejection I am feeling. For the first three days, it was as if a heavy boulder had been placed upon my chest and I could hardly breathe. I labored to breathe without hyperventilating. I felt as though I could vomit at any moment. That feeling lingered all week as well. Utter and complete rejection was all I could feel. And I hurt so badly that my heart literally hurt and was in pain. My heart was so broken, it actually ached.

For weeks, it was as if the Holy Spirit was grieving within me. Literally grieving. I had been unable to even speak at times. I would just cry uncontrollably for no apparent reason. I was upset, but I wasn't exactly sure why. I felt my husband was being dishonest with me, only I didn't know why. And finally, on Mother's Day, I found out. I woke up burdened and upset. I cried in private all morning. And when I got to church, I had to go hide in the bathroom. I got to hear all of two minutes of Sunday School class. Just long enough to find out what a friend's husband had done for her on Mother's Day already. It was so sweet and romantic. My husband had not even said the words, "Happy Mother's Day" to me yet. He called after he went to church earlier and I just knew he was going to tell me then. But he didn't. It turned out that he had forgotten something at home and wanted me to bring it to him. It was a book, I think. Well, he did forget something at home that day, but it wasn't just a book. It was me.

After Sunday School, I dragged him into his office and cried to him. He wanted to know what was wrong with me. And I couldn't tell him. All I could say was, "You didn't wish me a Happy Mother's Day." Of course, he thought I was insane and said I hadn't given him a chance yet. He teaches Sunday school, among other things. He's a busy man always helping other people. Isn't that what preachers are supposed to do? I think he just forgot he had a wife. So I brought the book and myself to church on Sunday. Somehow I managed to make it through the service.

Most of the day is a blur. That is, until the dreaded phone call. He met with her husband at the church that afternoon. And after a long time, he called to say he was on his way home. He sounded different and very upset. I wanted to know what was wrong. And he said he would be home soon. I was worried about him, so I demanded to know what was wrong. And he told me. He admitted to having an affair.

My entire world came crashing down. I dropped the phone and fell on my knees screaming and crying, "No!" I just remember thinking, "This is not real. This cannot be happening to me. No!" Everything became distant. My baby was crying and my five-year old was asking me what was wrong. I couldn't breathe. And I had this horrible pain in my chest. I couldn't speak. I could barely walk, and I was shaking all over. And then he came home.

He began apologizing profusely. He fell on his knees in front of me crying and begging for forgiveness. He grabbed my hand and asked me not to leave him. I pulled my hand away. I didn't want him to touch me. I didn't even want to look at him. I was so angry and hurt and then the questions began. Questions I'm not sure I really wanted the answers to, but I asked them anyway. I don't really know why. I sat numbly for a while, then went to my room and began packing a bag. I called my boss and told her I would not be in the next day and wasn't really sure about the day after that either. I told Kenneth we were leaving. We were going home. I wanted to see my parents. I didn't care where we slept that night, but I wasn't spending one more night in that house. He did exactly what I said.

That was the longest drive of my life. The tears came. And then the silence. Then some more questions. And after the answers, more tears. That vicious cycle continued all the way home. My husband had called some pastor friends of ours, and asked if we could meet with them. We did, and they were sweet, but I was so numb, I can't remember much. Except, "Beauty from ashes." (Isaiah 61:3) That was the scripture she gave me. I hope I can still believe that. I don't have much energy. The pain is too strong. And I am too weak. I can't eat. My stomach is so sick and I am a nervous wreck. Who knew a broken heart could have such a physical reaction. Amazingly enough I am still breathing. They say, what doesn't kill you only makes you stronger. We'll see.

On Monday, we met with our pastor to tell him and to resign. That was fun. (Sarcasm is one of my gifts.) I was crying before we even went in the door. And I was crying when we left. But amazingly enough, I'm still breathing. On the way home, I heard a song on the radio for the first time. It was called, "You Raise Me Up" by Selah. It moved me to tears. The kind of tears where your whole body shakes. I know that song was for me. God does love me and sent me that song. If I ever get through this, it will only be by the grace of God.

2

To Forgive or Not to Forgive

May 15

    I have now gone through every emotion imaginable. Deep valleys -- so deep I didn't know they even existed. And even a few peaks -- times when I truly believe everything will be okay and "this too shall pass." Right now, I really believe it will. Tomorrow, we have to tell the church and resign. I'm really not looking forward to that. I don't really know what to expect. I know what I'm hoping. I'm hoping SHE'S not there. Or maybe I'm hoping she is. I believe there are a few things I would like to say to her. Perhaps I don't need to speak to her but part of me wants to know if she's even remotely remorseful for what she's done to me.

    I know in my heart that it takes two and she is not the only one to blame, but I go over and over the details and conversations in my mind and I wonder, "What was she thinking?" What went through her mind as she tried to build a "friendship" with me, all the while betraying my trust? I've had time to cry and talk and scream at my husband and I know he is truly remorseful. I have not had that chance with her and I know she has "no godly remorse" as some say. The only justice would be if she were not allowed to attend church there until she's ready for counseling and to be sorry for what she's done.

It kills me to think they can continue to attend our church and receive all the love and compassion from our friends that I so desperately need but can't have. There's a certain amount of anger -- toward both of them -- when I think about how much I don't deserve this. I have pondered in my head what I could have possibly done to deserve this. I think sometimes I could've done or said something differently. But would've, should've, could'ves will be the death of me if I allow them to continue. Sometimes I want so desperately to just cry, but the tears won't come. In that same respect, I'm so exhausted, but I can't seem to find sleep. And when I do doze off, I have terrible dreams about her. So I awaken, only to have my mind run uncontrollably away with thoughts, fears, and mental images that hurt me all over again.

I know I need to forgive, but frankly, I don't want to. I really and truly don't even know if I can. Forgiving seems like such a hard thing to do and will require much energy. Energy I'm not sure I have. Forgive, or not to forgive? That is the question. And the answer…whatever…

3

...And a Funeral

May 19

My grandfather died today.

When it rains, it pours. I can't breathe again. I am suffocating with pain, and now grief. I want to be able to comfort my dad during this time, but I'm still just trying to wake up every morning. My grandfather was a great man. He loved God with all his heart and was a great preacher; raising three preachers of his own. He loved to tease and joke around. He was always good for a laugh. I'm sure he was a great father too. No doubt where my daddy learned how to be such a great father.

Most men wouldn't have been so forgiving of their daughter's husband after admitting to him of cheating on her. My dad opened his arms and his home and said, "If there's anything we can do to help, just ask." My parents are so great like that. They both probably wanted to kill my husband, but instead loved on him and reminded him of God's great mercy and forgiveness. I want to be just like them when I grow up. ☺

So now we have a funeral to plan. Doesn't the Bible say God will not put on us more than we can bear? I really believe He is giving me too much credit here. Maybe it's time we talked about this. Surely He is mistaken on exactly how much I can bear. Yet amazingly enough, I'm still breathing.

I feel like I'm in the middle of a really bad dumb blonde joke. Having to remind myself to breathe in and breathe out. Breathe in. Breathe out. Why is this so complicated? Because my husband cheated on me and my grandfather died. I wish I could bury the pain, but you have to "deal" to "heal".

Burying the pain would only grow bitterness. I don't want that. I just hope I can find the strength to overcome. All I know is that I cannot do this on my own.

"Jesus, please help me. I need you. The pain is unbearable. When will I feel relief? Please help my family, since I am of no help right now. Send your comforter to them…and to me."

4

Joy and Forgiveness

May 26

"I'm afraid I've lost my joy, and I can't seem to find it anywhere. I can't find any reason to look for it either."

These are words I remember speaking to him just days ago during one of my many meltdowns. I have such a strong desire to be an over comer and not be bitter or cold or hard. But it seems I don't have that strong desire to actually DO the things I need to do to make that happen. Other things I've said to him sound a bit like this, "I would rather DIE than go through this kind of pain again." And for right now -- I believe this is a very true statement. Of course, when I become "stable" again, I realize this would be awful for my family, especially my little girls, so then I want to live again. I can think of no greater betrayal than this. I believe if the "infidel" could feel this pain for only a moment, he would never be an infidel again, or perhaps he would not have gone there in the first place.

And I don't want to even think about the "other woman". Of course I have other words -- more accurate words -- in my head that will hopefully never reach the end of my pen and find its way onto this paper. So for now, we'll call her the "other woman" and leave it at that. I fear that I won't reach closure as far as she's concerned. And sometimes I want to talk to her and see her. Although the last time I saw her, I had a violent physical reaction that I don't want to ever relive. Just thinking about it makes me nauseous all over again. I keep thinking if only there was some remorse on her end. Some kind of apology or guilt for what she's done -- then maybe I could forgive her much more easily. But there is none, from what I've seen and heard. I suppose this is what "separates the women from the girls." This is a test of true forgiveness. I have forgiven my husband, the infidel, already. That now seems easy compared to this. This is forgiveness where forgiveness is undeserved; forgiveness with no strings attached. Pure and simple, forgiveness. But I suppose if we all got what we deserved; none of us would be forgiven at all. And yet the gift of forgiveness is offered to us all. Even as I write this, I struggle, knowing forgiveness is a gift. I do not want to GIVE anything to this woman who has so callously taken -- stolen -- so many things from me. But isn't the Bible clear about when a thief comes to steal from you, give him your coat too? And doesn't the Lord's Prayer say, "Forgive us our sins, for we also forgive everyone who sins against us," (Luke 11:4)?

"I know this is your will, O Lord. And I know what being out of your will feels like so please help me forgive this woman and replace my hatred for her with a Godly love. I don't want to be her friend. I just want to be healed. And I know that bitterness and anger have no healing properties whatsoever. In fact, they have the exact opposite effect; something I've said from the very beginning that I don't want."

What an awesome testimony if I allow God to forgive her through me. Just knowing that if she's repented at all, God has already forgiven her and oh, how I want to be like Christ. I am finding new things He is to me through this trial. I'm always amazed at how He reveals Himself so clearly in order to comfort, encourage, and show Himself mighty in times like these. I believe I'm supposed to write a letter to the "other woman" during our restoration period. Perhaps my book can be my letter. And she will know about my forgiveness.

So why is there still some part of me that wants to hate her and hold a grudge for what she's done? I recognize this part of me all too well. Its name is "flesh". Hello flesh. Always resurfacing just when I think I've won; a constant battle between my spirit and my flesh. Paul writes so vividly about that struggle... that which I know to do, I do not, (Romans 7:15-25) I've really got to read my Bible more. There are little treasures hidden in the pages. Although they're not really hidden, are they? The first time I read this passage I said, "Huh?" However, over the years I have understood quite clearly what it means. The bible says to crucify my flesh daily. So I may be forgiving her daily for a while until my flesh gives up the struggle. Today I choose to forgive. Goodbye flesh.

For the first time since D-Day, or Discovery Day, or the day I found out, my thoughts have not turned to her. I am not at this moment dwelling on her or imagining her with my husband. In fact, I wish to never put those two together in a sentence again. They do not belong together in a sentence or in any other way, for that matter. Hey, the Bible says I must forgive -- it doesn't say I need to encourage the unforgiving behavior. No, I must forgive or neither will my Father forgive me (Matthew 6:15).

And no one is without sin (Romans 3:23).

And no one with sin can enter into the kingdom of Heaven (I Corinthians 6:9 & 10).

I can see the sun peeking out through the cracks in my blinds…literally and metaphorically. Now that the sun is awake, maybe rest will find me. "Come unto me, all who are weary and burdened, and I will give you rest. Take my yoke upon you and learn from me, for I am gentle and humble in heart, and you will find rest for your souls," (Matthew 11:28).

It just occurred to me that the sun is always awake; we just can't always see it. The clouds sometimes "cloud" our view. And the darkness of night covers the light of the sun. But joy comes in the morning (Psalm 30:5). So maybe I didn't lose my joy after all. Maybe joy just took a "sabbatical."

5

Fairy Tales & Optimism

June 8

Tomorrow will be exactly one month since D-Day. And tonight as I lay here desperately seeking sleep, it feels like I just found out yesterday. The pain is still as fresh as it was on that dreadful day. Although I am able to write now and also breathe as well, two things I could not do right away, I replay the details of that day over and over in my mind and it is as if I am running into the knife that stabbed me so brutally again. Forgive and forget, right? The forgiving part is a piece of cake compared to the forgetting part.

There are still so many nights, like tonight, where sleep is the farthest thing from me and I look over at him and wonder how it is that he can sleep so peaceably. Relief, perhaps? Relief that it's exposed. No more lying and sneaking around. I'm sure the use of so much energy must really drain a person. And now I know; I forgive, and he can rest. For the first time in our marriage, I feel that no amount of sharing with each other can make us understand each others' feelings. I do not know what he is feeling or thinking at this moment. I do not attempt to imagine the grief and sorrow of losing everything: job, friends, etc. And the extreme amount of guilt that must accompany betrayal. And I know he can't possibly feel the hurt and rejection I experience daily caused by his betrayal; which I can only compare to death.

My 5-year-old daughter was extremely wise when she told my parents she thought someone had died. A pain any worse than the one experienced and I would have laid dead. At times I am amazed I have lived through such hell. Torture this harsh should only be reserved for hell itself and the demons that belong there. How did they manage to free themselves for one day and cast a piece of hell into my world? My world? Perhaps that was my first problem. I do not have a world. Not one in which I am in control, anyway. Because if I had written this chapter in my life, the outcome, I assure you, would have been completely different....

> "For when the knight in shining armor was propositioned by the wicked witch disguised as a beauty, he pulls from his pocket the white scarf that he carries near his heart. A white handkerchief which symbolizes the purity of the vow he made to return to his beautiful princess bride who has kept herself pure awaiting his return from battle. As he waves the white handkerchief in front of the temptress, he firmly says no to her seductive ways and rides off in the opposite direction to return to his bride as quickly as his trusty steed will carry him, never once regretting his decision to remain faithful to his future queen."

I realize that this passage from my imaginary book in my imaginary world is a bit far-fetched, but a girl can dream, can't she? I remember it was not so long ago that I believed in fairy tales and I believed in happy endings. I also believed in "till death do us part" and "let no man (or woman) put asunder what God has joined together," (Mark 10:9). And I have never stopped believing that God put us together. There were so many times Satan tried to plant a thought that was not true. But I know my God and I know He told me this is the man that I was to marry. And Satan, other women, and not even my husband can change that. Sure, he can decide he doesn't want to be that man. But he can't change the fact that God chose him to be my mate. God gave him to me. He entrusted us with each other to be each other's helpmate. And to love each other until death do us part. And no one has died, at least not literally, so guess what? I'm not ready to give up on our marriage quite yet.

It is now morning, but only barely. I am trying to count how many hours of sleep I will get if I go to sleep this very moment. Not nearly enough. Writing my feelings helps so much more than dwelling on my thoughts. My thoughts get carried away so quickly, but it takes me too long to write (for my feelings to go that far). This entire trial has consumed my thoughts and now my dreams as well. Even if I could find sleep, I would only be awakened by yet another dream reminding me of how painful reality is. I know my husband fears that I will retaliate or "get even" as he has put it. And perhaps that fear is good for him now. But this has been such a painful thing. I cannot imagine if I had to go through it alone. At least I can go to his arms after I scream out in rage at him or bitingly allow my anger to escape; which seems to happen more often than not. At least with him here, I can receive a loving hug, a sweet embrace or a soft brush of a kiss followed by an apology and a reaffirming of his love for me. There have been times when I doubted that love because I didn't understand how someone could love someone so much and hurt them so badly.

But I also know the blinding power of sin and the hold it can have on a person and I believe him when he says the blinders fell off his eyes when he confessed his sin to me and he could finally see me for what I was and what he almost lost or threw away. He's lucky that I do not like to be thrown away.

I am that stubborn gum that sticks to the side of the garbage can when you are trying to empty it. No matter how hard you try, you just can't get it off and it ends up sticking to everything. The more you try to remove it, the more stubborn it gets until finally it is covering everything, leaving its sticky mark on everything as if to say, "I will not go away! You can't get rid of me that easily!"

A heavy exhaustion has come over my eyes suddenly. If I thought there was a chance of sleep, I would put down this pen immediately but I fear the exhaustion I feel now is merely a tease; another ploy to get me to close my eyes and think on these things that are not beautiful, holy, or pure, but horrible, evil, and dirty. And unfortunately, that's truth and reality right now.

Someone very wise once said, "Life sucks and then you die." I never wanted to believe that to be a true statement and yet I find myself believing it at times. And just when I think I'm about to cross the line over to being cynical, the little girl in me emerges. You know, the one who believes dreams really do come true, fairy tales do happen, and oh yeah, the glass really is half full. That's me. That's who I am. And hopefully my husband will see, know, and love me for that.

Some people think that is a weakness or a sign of ignorance and immaturity. Well I might just be dumb enough to believe that everything will be okay. I rest in God's promises. "I can do all things through Christ who strengthens me," (Philippians 4:13). And… "If ye ask anything in my name, it shall be done," (John 14:14). And… "He brings beauty from ashes, strength for fear, gladness for mourning, peace for despair," (Isaiah 61:3).

I gave him predictability,
When he wanted something different.

I gave him security,
When he wanted excitement.
I gave him love,
When he wanted lust.
I gave him me,
And he wanted someone else.

How's that for a freakin' Hallmark card?! Next poem in this series entitled: "Screw You!" Just kidding! I have to laugh to keep from crying.

6

Stupid vs. Trusting

June 12

It is 12:56 a.m. Once again I cannot sleep. The little sleep fairy forgot to sprinkle me with her dust tonight. Maybe it's because I'm so short that she keeps overlooking me. ☺ Anyway, I wanted to write because I am struggling with feeling stupid. I keep thinking how stupid I must be to not notice what was going on. To have this going on right under my nose and not even know about it. Is that just stupidity on my part? Or maybe I was just being trusting.

I trusted my husband and did believe everything he told me. Right near the end I caught him in a couple of discrepancies. Things he didn't even need to lie about. And I thought he was being dishonest but I didn't know why. Now everything makes perfect sense. Hindsight really is 20/20. But I tell you the truth when I say, I was completely blind sided by this news. I could not have been more shocked by any other revelation than one of this nature. I could feel him growing distant but I didn't know why and he wouldn't talk to me about it, except to say he was stressed or tired. It got to the point where everything was, "I'm just stressed." Or "I'm tired."

He used to love doing things with me. We really were not separated much at all. Until eventually I felt he just wanted to get away from me. I even felt like he didn't want to sit by me at church anymore. He always had someone to go talk to or an errand to run or something in the office to take care of.

I guess my biggest problem at this moment is that I was replaced, when I should have been irreplaceable. I was unwanted for something only I should have been wanted for. A role that only I should have filled was so casually filled by another. A desire only I should fulfill was fulfilled by someone else, a stranger really. Not that a close acquaintance would have made the situation any better. No, in fact that would have been much worse. We did not enter into our vows lightly. And for something that took much thought and prayer to enter into, seems just as much consideration would have gone into throwing it all away.

Then there is the fact that my husband confessed to me only because he got caught. And what if he had not gotten caught? How long would he have continued this charade? He said he would not have told me because he did not want to hurt me. I think that to be more than just a little ironic. The one thing that could have hurt me the worst is the one thing he chose to do; the worst betrayal -- at best. So was I just too trusting, or too stupid? There are so many things I did not expect from my husband. I did not expect wealth. I thought love was enough. Although I now completely understand the phrase, "First time marry for love, second time marry for money." Sometimes love just isn't quite enough, is it? And that completely screws up my whole fairy-tale mentality. How can everything come up roses when you're constantly being suffocated by all the weeds?

And unless you aggressively rip out all those nasty weeds, they will overtake and kill your beautiful garden. I'm planting new flowers now, and being vigilant about those weeds. First sign of a weed, and I'm grabbing hold with both hands, yanking as hard as I can with all my might, and removing that intruding eyesore.

Speaking of plants, when I went to our old home on Thursday to take care of some business, which was very painful, I saw our little rock at the front of our garden that reads, "God Bless Our Home." And during a surge of rage, I wanted very badly to pick up that rock and crush it and toss it to the road. It's not like I don't want God to bless our home, because I do and I believe He can and will. It's just that I felt He tried to bless us and my husband carelessly threw it back at Him. And maybe a small part of me was angry at God for not protecting us better from the attack of the enemy. I mean, this is certainly no blessing. And as badly as my husband wanted something else, I wanted us to be a family and be blessed. So why is it that his wants and desires got fulfilled but mine did not?

Back to my expectations. I did not expect my husband to change. I accepted him—all of him—including his faults. I was just hoping he could do the same for me. I've beaten myself up over the last few days about what I could have done differently. How I could have changed. And yes, there are ways I could have changed. I know it angered him to ask me to and not see it. But there were things I asked of him that I never saw. I wanted him to have more patience with me and my daughter. To not be so short-fused. To cut back on some things so we wouldn't have to come last, to name a few. I guess I thought if he wasn't going the extra mile for me, why should I bother? I already did so many things. Some things he will never even know about. Like our towels. Every time I would get a shower, I took a ratty old towel so that when my husband got ready to shower, he could have the big fluffy one.

I know that seems trivial, but it is just one example of putting him first. A couple of times we were almost out of contact solution and I would ration my drops to just barely enough to wet my contacts so that he would have all he needed. Or I would just toss that pair and open a new pair the next day. And now I think to myself—why? Why did I do those things? He didn't know I was doing them. I never told him. I didn't want to tell him. I just wanted to love him in every aspect of my life even if he didn't see.

I think partly I wanted to be submissive and I thought by putting him first I was exhibiting that submissiveness. Now what? What do I say to all those cynics who thought of my submissiveness as a weakness? The strong-willed women who think because I'm staying, I'm a weaker woman somehow. But who really is weaker? The one who runs at the first sign of a challenge and gives up when things make the situation hard? Or is the strong one the one who endures to the end? The one who keeps her promise no matter how mistreated or betrayed?

The easy thing would be to run. Jesus never said, "Well, I know I came to save the world but these people are just too mean to me and they've hurt my feelings, so I think I'll just go back home and sit on my throne where it's easy." If you think He did, then you are reading the wrong book. My Jesus suffered the ridicule, persecution, and crucifixion, and endured to the end. And He is the strongest man I know. So to the ones who say, "I told you so…," I say, "Maybe; but I'm strong and I'm stronger for it. People change and I will display the greatest strength in allowing forgiveness to flow through me." Although this decision is not permission granted for a repeat offense. No, I'm afraid the consequences for such an act would be most severe.

"And I bind up Satan in the name of Jesus. I pray protection and a hedge about our family and our marriage. And I pray that God bind us together with cords that cannot be broken. In

Jesus' name. Amen."

Somewhere, deep down, no matter how insecure I get, I know that my husband loves me and it has been quite nice to hear him say so out loud. It boosts my confidence and builds my security back up brick by brick. I go back and forth from completely insecure to totally self-confident. One moment I want to become anorexic and buy a new wardrobe and the next minute I want to say, "I don't need you. I'm beautiful." And buy a new wardrobe. ☺ I think it's some twisted way of building myself up. Maybe I'm afraid he won't tell me enough that I'm pretty and he loves me. So I tell myself. I'm constantly fishing for compliments and I don't even realize I do it until after the fact. And if I don't get the compliment I want, I just tell him how good I look. Some psychologist would have a field day with this one, I know.

I notice other women do it too. I wonder why. Extreme insecurity? I know some of them are insecure. But I was raised knowing I was loved and to be secure. My husband hasn't exactly been free with the compliments. He's too busy mostly and I've told myself that for so long that I'm even making excuses for him in my journal.

No one should ever be too busy for their family. Including me, which is another reason I don't want to work outside the home. I want to be there for my family. I want to fill my home with prayers and make it a safe refuge that my family will want to come home to. I want my daughters to feel safe and secure, and my husband to feel it is a haven of rest so that he will not want to retreat somewhere else…or with someone else. I want to be the best wife and mother that I can be.

I guess that's why this is even more personal. But I felt that if I was a good enough wife, then he wouldn't have wanted to stray. I get very little comfort in knowing other men envied my husband, because I wonder why I wasn't good enough for him.

I guess I always had insecurity about the whole sex thing because I had never been with anyone else before. And since he had not wanted anyone else prior, I assumed I was okay in this area. But now I know he obviously did want someone else in this area, so maybe I'm not okay at all. Sure he gets satisfied every time, but men need sex like they need food and water, so it seems they would eventually be fulfilled, right? It's hard for me to understand this sexual addiction thing.

Did I forget to mention that? During one of our counseling sessions, my husband admitted to sexual addiction. An addiction that dates back to when he was 11 and a neighbor introduced him to hard-core pornography. An addiction that ultimately led to the adulterous relationship. I'm hoping this is something counseling will help with. I know my husband said it was just an addiction and I shouldn't take it personal, but it is very personal. Probably the most personal thing and now it's not the same. There are just no words to describe it. Yet I continue to try. So much so that my hand is about to fall off. I really want to go to sleep. It's 2:40 a.m. now and I'm thinking, "10 more pages and it'll be time to get up!" Let me just write that I love my husband dearly and I'm committed to him and to this marriage. And by the grace of God, we will survive and not only survive, but prosper! In Jesus' name!!

"Dear Lord, please help me sleep! In Jesus' name, Amen. P.S. Please heal me, Lord. It hurts so bad."

7

His Hands & A Treasure

June 27

It has been one week since Father's Day. Father's Day was not too terribly difficult. Not nearly as bad as I expected it to be. We did celebrate the day before since we were so busy on Sunday driving 11 hours home from our family reunion in Abilene. Perhaps that helped. It sort of took my mind off briefly. Except for a few fits, I was mostly okay. Thankfully, we were alone in the car and I could vent as much and as often as needed.

It's kind of funny -- I know I've got to get these things out, but I always feel so bad about dragging him back through it all. I mean, I certainly don't want him to think about it or HER on a regular basis. Lord knows I would like to just forget about the whole thing. I know you're supposed to deal with it when it comes up or it will never go away, but I also think there's a fine line between dealing with it and obsessing over it. I need counseling. Or a miracle from God. Perhaps both.

"Please Lord, help me heal!"

I don't want her to be a part of my marriage any longer. Yet by continually thinking of her, I feel like I'm keeping her in my marriage and in my husband's life. My whole life I've always believed that when you make love to a person, you become one with that person. The fact that I was the one he married somehow sets me apart from all the other women in his life. Our vows are what made me somehow different -- special. And then he forsook me and those vows and I have nothing to make me feel special. Sure he says he loves me. He said he loved me before. He says I'm beautiful. Many women are beautiful. He thought she was beautiful. I somehow told myself and even believed myself when I said I was different. I was special. Was I so arrogant to think I was too special to not be replaced? What was so special about me to keep him home? Nothing, I suppose.

And then I have to remember that this is yet another tactic of the enemy. The devil would like me to think that. Just like he had my husband blinded by his own sin and now he is a new man: a clean, repentant man who no longer has anything to hide. I guess it's the human nature in me that gets the two confused at times. I have forgiven, but I have not forgotten. I'm not sure that will ever happen. Although I pray to God that it will.

"Please help me forget."

A mind is a terrible thing to waste -- on bad memories!!!

I used to love to look at my husband's hands. I don't know if he remembers, but it was one of the first things I found attractive about him. They are beautiful, yet manly. The most perfect hands I have seen. And when they caress my face or brush hair from my eyes, I grow weak in the knees like a smitten school girl. Now, occasionally, when I look at his perfect hands, I see all the imperfectness of his affair, knowing that those hands that I love were holding another woman. Maybe even caressing her face or brushing the hair away from her eyes...or worse. I am wincing now from the pain of the very thought. Yet I see at times the same hands that I love, that love me. Even now as I gaze at those two hands, I do not flinch, but desire instead. I desire assurance mostly. Assurance of his love for me and a promise it will not happen again. The scary thing is that I cannot expect or demand such a promise.

This week was especially difficult. I felt as if I had come so far and things were so much better and then this week happened. A flood of memories I thought were starting to fade came violently flooding back. I kept replaying the moment I found out and the deep unbearable pain it caused. I could not even stand. The physical reaction was so intense I had no idea a hole was actually being created in my heart. I have known no other pain like this before. And I pray I never do again. My pain is very much in proportion with the love I have for my husband. This will motivate me to heal. This morning at church I prayed that God would make me beautiful in my husband's eyes and mold me into a treasure of a wife for him to have. I want to be a beautiful jewel to him. I want him to be proud to call me his bride and, in spite of all my faults, to know that I am God's gift to him just as he is God's gift to me.

I have kept things over the years; some would say I am a packrat. Most of the items are virtually worthless and priceless at the same time. I have some old costume jewelry my great-grandmother gave me and some glued together construction paper with my daughter's handwriting on it. A home made card, I think.

But if I had a safe, these things would be in it. Not because of the money they are worth: they are worth none. But they are priceless. I want to be that old costume jewelry or the two pieces of glued construction paper. Full of infinite flaws and worth nothing, but priceless in my husband's eyes, just as I am precious in God's eyes.

"Is that possible, Oh Lord? Can you make me a jewel to my husband while I am here on Earth? I want to treasure him as well. I want to prosper in our relationship and show your mighty work and prove you to be the awesome God I know you are. I love you, Lord. Amen."

8

Hangover, Sympathy & Impatience

July 7

One step forward...10 steps back!

Wow. Yesterday sucked!

I thought it was supposed to get better, not worse. Actually, I thought I was better and then...BAM! I was knocked flat on my back again. I was so depressed that I cried all day. I just laid there. I thought if I could just sleep then I would at least not have to think about it for a few hours.

I went back over every conversation and replayed every situation; even the ones I wasn't there for, if you know what I mean. I even created a few new conversations in my head. You know -- what I would say if I ever bump into her again. What I would've done if I had been there or "walked in" on the few occasions I was not invited to. I believe they have a word for that—it's called "OBSESSION." And it's not the perfume. There's nothing sweet-smelling about this obsession.

I sometimes wish I could talk to her even though we're not to have any contact with them at all. But then I don't know what I would say, so I quickly change my mind. All the insecurities I've felt over the last two months came flooding back to me, which makes me angry. I was the most confident I have ever been in my life; before the exposure to the affair. I was finally comfortable in my skin.

Boy, Satan had every aspect of this thing worked out, didn't he? "Like a roaring lion, seeking whom he may devour." (I Peter 5:8) On top of all the emotional stuff, as if that's not enough, we could possibly lose our house, car and anything else we semi-own, if something good financially doesn't happen soon. So all in all, life's a bowl of cherries!

And today, I feel like I have a hangover. I don't really know what that feels like since I've never had a hangover. But if I had to guess, this would be it: horrible headache, light sensitivity, and all I want to do is sleep. Add to that the normal once-a-month female symptoms and you've got yourself a real party!

I sound like the bitter old women I detest so much, whose husbands cheated on them. You know, the ones I so desperately do NOT want to become. What's funny is that I find myself sympathizing with those women now. I used to get angry with how they treated their men, but now I understand. How can I argue with them when I feel the same way? The only problem is that's how they justify their actions. I don't want to have those "actions"; let alone be able to justify them. How can I be different? And I listen to those women. Years later they are still so mean to their husbands but now I feel their pain, and I understand their hurt. Does it ever heal? You don't want to hurt your husband, but your defenses automatically go up as if to try and protect yourself from hurting anymore. But you can't protect yourself. As much as I beat myself up for what happened, I could not have stopped it. I don't think. Enough of that. I could go crazy wondering about that.

I had to look up some rates on the computer for a Motel 6. On the main page is a picture of one of the rooms and I couldn't help but wonder was this THE room? And then I got a full visual in my mind which was a little more than torturous. Have you ever imagined the man you love in the arms of another woman and then known it really happened? There are no words (although the mental images are quite enough).

Since I'm writing this to no one, I would guess that no, you have not imagined or experienced it. It's funny. I usually write to God or to myself or pretend I'm writing my book. But tonight I'm writing to my journal -- an inanimate object. Not only that, but I'm asking you questions, as if you could possibly answer. I'm sure there's a word for that…insanity, perhaps? ☺

I'm ready to go to counseling. I'm ready to get healed. I'm ready for my husband to get healed. I'm ready for us to move on. I'm ready to sell our house. I'm ready to buy a new one. I'm ready for my husband to get a full-time job. I'm ready for the devil to leave us alone. I'm ready for the Lord to come back and take me away. I'm ready to wake up tomorrow from this horrible nightmare and realize that's all it was -- a nightmare. I am NOT, however, ready to wait!

"Lord, teach me to be like you.
Teach me your ways.
Teach me to grow
And heal me along the way.
Amen."

9

Passionate Love & Ohio Questions

July 12

We just made love. The hot, passionate kind when you can't keep your hands off each other. It reminds me of the kind of love-making we had when we conceived our second child. That was right before everything went to hell. But tonight was sweeeeet! And I don't mean sweet in a "school-girlish" sense. It's more like a "guys' locker room" sense. Good thing journals are meant for my eyes only! (Oops, ☺).

Today was such an emotional flip-flop. One minute I was great, the next minute I was crying. Everything reminds me of what happened. On the way home tonight from church, I cried because I couldn't believe it had actually happened. It was really true. My husband was really with another woman and I couldn't change that. And it wasn't like he was raped. He wanted her. That's the sorry part. He *wanted* her. So I cried. Then when I got home, my brother and his wife were there and I cracked jokes and laughed my head off for a while. Then, all of a sudden, I wanted to cry again. Then I wanted to make love. Even *I* don't know what emotion I will have from one moment to the next.

    I have decided on a few questions I would like to ask the counselor when we go to Ohio in two weeks:
    1. How come every time my husband is remotely critical of me now, I lose it completely? I want to tell him, "Why doesn't he just go find Blondie? I'm sure she can do it better!" And that's the LAST thing I want. I just immediately get defensive and hurt. Will I ever get over that and how? Like the other day when he didn't have any brown socks clean and he was upset. I was thinking to myself, "I'm sure Ding Dong's maid would love to wash your socks for you!" What I said out loud was, "At least I wash laundry and I don't get some hired help to do it." I feel like I'm always in competition with her. And that brings me to question two:
    2. Why do I always feel like I'm in competition with her? Every time my husband and I talk about her or the situation, I feel the need to tell him I don't sit on my butt watching soaps and smoking cigarettes all day. I don't have any tattoos and I don't hire a maid to clean my house for me.

    Why do I need to make myself look better than her? I know it's a huge insecurity and I feel like she somehow "won" my man. Because he chose her over me and I cannot describe that kind of rejection. There are no words. There are several more questions I need to remember to ask but I am so exhausted at this moment, it will just have to wait.

    "Please help my baby sleep all night, Oh Lord. I need some rest. Lots of rest. Thank you. And please sell our home and heal our hearts. In Jesus' name, Amen."

10

Motel 6 & The Holy Spirit

July 21

    We leave in two days to go to Ohio. I can't wait. Finally, we will get some counseling and maybe even some answers. Yesterday was quite hard. We passed a Motel 6 on our way home from church and I cried the rest of the way. The loud, uncontrollable kind of cry that you cannot contain nor try to hide. My face was so red and puffy by the time we arrived home that everyone noticed.

    This morning I was so angry at God. At God -- of *all* people, God. As if He actually had some part in my pain. I was so angry at Him because I felt He was not answering my prayers anymore. I had just gotten off the phone with the bank. It was not a productive or pleasant conversation. I asked my mother how come nothing good ever happens to us. It seems like one bad thing after another. I am rather weary of bad news. And I have grown quite tired of ill fate. I am more than ready for some good news. I am ready for God to kick the devil's butt on my behalf. To punch his lights out and say, "That one's for Tara." I felt like God didn't want to help me. I know that is not true. After I repented -- several times -- I heard a song on the radio that made me cry and all of the sudden, the Spirit began to well up inside of me and I began to speak in the spirit. In my car!!! I had to turn off the radio so I could pray. It was so wonderful. I know He loves me and cares for me. Then I read, "The Prayer of Jabez," by Bruce Wilkinson. So now I believe it's okay to pray for a blessing. So here goes:

"Lord, please bless me and my family. I love you."

I really must go to sleep now before I pass out.

"Thank you God for your love. And thank you for the healing that I know will come. Please keep us safe on our trip and speak to me on the way. "
Love, T.

11

Salty Tears & Murky Swamps

July 23

Last night, after making love, my husband kissed me. And I wondered if he could taste the salt from the tears that ran onto my lips. The Bible says that God bottles up the tears we cry, (Psalm 56:8). I wonder how many bottles He's collected of mine. Are the heavens going to run out of bottles soon? Perhaps God will change His mind about keeping all of mine. I wonder if the bottles are labeled. And I wonder how many bottles came from the past two months alone.

Two months. At times it feels as if it has been much longer than two months and other times, it still feels like it was yesterday. Although I can be glad it was not yesterday. I would not be able to write if it were. Simple tasks, such as writing, were not so easy then. In fact daily tasks, such as feeding the children and getting dressed, I found most difficult. Today I got my clothes on without thinking on it. I consider that a miracle. I am making progress, although I'm not sure I would have said that last night. Something came over me. The memories came back. The insecurities first, quickly followed by the crippling pain. A pain so sharp and deadly, it feels as though a sword were piercing my heart, making it once again hard to breathe. Is death worse than this?

It must be, although I cannot imagine a pain any worse. It's no wonder elderly people soon pass away after losing a loved one that they've shared their life with for about 50 years. Or even five years. When you become one with someone and promise your life to them, it is a bond like no other. Indescribable, really. That's why it is so painful to think that after making such a promise, he freely became one with someone else. She is always there. In my quiet time, she appears. When we make love, she is there. She is always there haunting my dreams and invading my life. And making me cry salty tears after making love to my husband. MY husband. I did not know such feelings of insecurity, jealousy, and despair could all exist inside of me. We are on our way to Akron at this moment. I hope the counselor next week can help.

"Please God, send us some help. I know three days are not quite long enough to tackle the mountains of emotional trauma that we bring. But I know you can do anything. And I believe you can use a counselor to help heal us and also to fix us. Please let this trip go well and let us all get along. Thank you. I love you. Amen."

We are driving through Louisiana now. Beautiful simple land. Lots of sunshine and a…murky swamp!?! I love all those old movies made here in Louisiana. Old plantation homes. Southern accents. I do not, however, like the movies made here such as, "Swamp Thing". My fear of alligators ranks right up there with my fear of snakes. Not to mention the ugliness of a swamp. How plantation homes and swamps can coexist for so long amazes me.

My life reminds me of Louisiana. Up until this point, I have sauntered around the front porch of my plantation home—pretty, pleasant, and nearly perfect. Only to step off my porch to find myself corset-high in a murky swamp. I suppose I will have to just remove my corset to keep my head above water and kick off my petticoat in order to out-swim the gators and snakes. The only question is…where do I go now? I can't stay here and be eaten alive. I can't go back to my porch. There's no longer security there. We've gone too far over the ledge. I'm just swimming now, to stay alive. And all around is nothing but swamp. I wonder how fast I can swim. The world is not completely covered in swamp. I see no end near…but that doesn't mean there is no end. Just not one in sight…yet! I know on the other side of a valley is a mountain. But what is on the other side of a swamp? The swamp appears worse than a valley. Perhaps heaven waits on the other side of this swamp. Or at least another plantation home -- with a much larger porch, of course. ☺

12

A Kiss & A Bandage

July 26

A kiss and a bandage. How many times have I heard my little girl say, "Ouch mommy. It hurts." And with a kiss and a bandage, the pain and tears cease. What is the miracle in the kiss and bandage? An immediate healer to all of life's little "boo-boo's". Sometimes when I pray, all I can say is "Ouch God. It hurts." And then I wait patiently for my kiss and bandage. And after I've shed a few tears and gotten a hug, I feel better for a time. But unfortunately, like my daughter, the band-aid is removed prematurely and the scab that had begun to form is scratched off, leaving the wound to bleed fresh again. And the kiss? It's all but forgotten.

We're in Ohio now. It's kind of funny because when all of this "hit the fan", so to speak, all I wanted to do was run away. Far away. Away from all the pain and the source of it. Not really away from my husband, and certainly not my children. As you know we ALL packed up and drove home to be with family. But I did want to run away from my house, our town, that woman and her family. But now that I'm several states away, I find the pain does not stay behind. It follows you, instead. Maybe at the counseling sessions, I can leave the pain here and I can return home; free from this smothering pain so I can breathe again without laboring. I remember when I could breathe without thinking and didn't have to work so hard at it. I miss that.

"Please Lord, use this week to heal us and fix us. Please help us to get all we possibly can and leave here a changed couple...for the better!
Love, T."

13

The Letter

July 28

The counselor says I should write a letter to the other woman, "evicting" her from my life. Is it that simple? Had I known that all it took was a letter, I would have written it long ago. I thought you just needed a punching bag, with a picture of her on it. I wonder if they will take it back now. Ha Ha!

There's no punching bag. That would intimidate me because they are too big. So a letter it is. A letter, I can do. You must know that names have been changed to protect the guilty. Here we go…

Delilah, (funny choice, huh?)
I will never understand how you could have betrayed me so. It is true that we were not very close friends, but I trusted you, nonetheless. I will never understand how

you could take advantage of the fact that I opened up MY home to you and your family only to have you shove it back into my face. I cannot fathom what kind of person can proposition MY husband while I am in the kitchen baking cookies for your children. I have said before that this kind of pain should only be reserved for hell itself and the demons that live there. It only makes sense that someone capable of inflicting such pain would somehow be related. And the fact that you have shown no remorse only validates my point. The depth at which you sank to make me believe you were shy, innocent, and mild-mannered -- everything you are not -- leads me to believe there is an overwhelming amount of evil in you. Not to mention a seriously severed conscious; if one exists at all. The uncanny way you manipulated and slithered your way into my home, my family, and my marriage. Not unlike the serpent -- a creature I have a large amount of hatred and disdain for. I could write pages on the pain you have caused me, but you would never understand it, nor would you even care perhaps. I know you cannot understand this hurt because you are incapable of feeling this hurt. You only understand causing it. I know this because you are capable of being hurt in proportion to how much you love. And no one loved my husband like I loved him. You are a woman, a wife, and mother but only by chance, not by bond. Because if you had loved your family half as much as a true wife and mother, you would have never considered such an act for the pain and suffering it causes families. No wife or mother who has an unconditional love for her family would risk that. And what kind of woman has sex with a stranger while her children sleep in the other room? I suppose you were lucky they did not have a bad dream and need you. Although I can't imagine them finding comfort and solace in your arms, so I'm sure they would not have gone to you anyway. But certainly you already knew that and therefore were not concerned. I would have worried about the devastating conversation I would have had if my child were to ask why a strange man was in my bed. But I guess someone who is not concerned with how much she hurts people, like you are, would not have had that worry. Things taken away only hurt by how valuable they are. If you had stolen my favorite T-shirt, I would not be writing this letter to you. But you did not steal my favorite T-shirt. You stole something much more valuable to me: my husband, my marriage, and at times, my sanity. You have invaded my thoughts, my dreams, and my alone time. So this letter is to let you know that I am coming to take back what you (the enemy) have stolen from me. You can no longer be a part of my marriage or my mind. You see, Delilah, when I put my trust in you as a friend, you signed a contract that my husband was off limits. But not only did you not keep that trust, you broke it and every other expectation a friend has. Not just a friend, but any semi-moral human being in existence. Adultery is not just a "no-no" on the Ten Commandments. It is a wrong recognized by all humans -- liberal or not. It is a betrayal of trust in the worst way. I could wish to get even with you, but you could never experience the fullness of my pain so don't worry about that. Besides, "Vengeance is mine, says the Lord." (Romans 12:19) And I could never do as good a job as He. I just wanted you to know I am "evicting" you out of my life. No longer will you have a place of torment within me. I won't allow it. You tried your best to destroy me, but I'm still here and we're still married. I have already begun the process. In the beginning, your name was "psycho witch" and now I refer to you as "ding dong". As in, "ding, dong the witch is dead." Ha! I can even say your name now without crying or wanting to throw something. You will no longer have control over me. And I will not allow you to rule any aspect of my life anymore. Every bad and ugly thing that has happened, we are working to turn around for good with God's help. Soon the name "Delilah" will be a distant memory with no ill-affect whatsoever. I will make sure, with God's help, that day will come! Goodbye Delilah.

Sincerely,
Tara

# 14

Closing on the House

August 19

Don't let my lack of journal entries fool you into thinking I am healed. I am not healed; just really busy and equally tired. We signed the papers on the house today. In fact, the money should be in our account by now. I have been very busy tying up loose ends for the sale of this house. And now it is over. Finished. Closed. Done. And I miss it already. Maybe I was too attached. I loved that home and having to sell it is just one more reminder of what happened.

Packing our house was extremely difficult. I wanted to cry and scream and cry some more. But I couldn't because people were there helping us. Although, I did have one little breakdown in front of my mother. It was when I was packing up my room. I threw away the sheets and cover. I even threw away the pillows. Who knows why? But I didn't want to risk having that home-wrecker on my pillows so even the new ones went into the trash. Good riddance! There were so many reminders there. Not just of the affair, but life leading up to it as well. It's good that we sold the house and are going to move. I didn't need to be there anymore anyway. So thus ended a chapter in my life. If it weren't for all those darn epilogues, I might could move on! ☺

So, now we need another house. I kind of liked the old one. I hope I'm not too spoiled. I have a feeling we will be "down-sizing" a bit. Just another sacrifice to save this marriage. I want to stay home with my children. So, we will all be sacrificing a bit. Please tell me it will be worth it all!

"Lord, please give us the wisdom to know what to do."

15

Writer's Block & Drunk Cowboys

August 22

I believe I have writer's block. I have stared at this page for several minutes, but to no avail. "Writer's Block" -- that's kind of like a woman having nothing to say, right? Ha! No, that can't be it. I could say plenty, but it would be rambling and not worth much of anything. I'm supposed to "Write it out. Talk it out. Pray it out." (A nifty tip I learned in counseling.) I want to write but I don't know what to say. I suppose I could pray.

"Dear Lord,
Please forgive us for missing church today. You know why
we did not go, but I still want to apologize. Today was nice,
leisurely spending time with the family and have nothing to do.
But I will try not to make it a habit. Thank you."

Every mother will appreciate this story. It is not for the weak of stomach, however. Last night, my daughter had a friend sleep over, and we were awakened at 2:00 a.m. when my daughter informed me that her friend had thrown up. I rushed into their room only to be knocked nearly unconscious by that dreaded odor and not to mention the sight that caused my own stomach to turn in displeasure. Several times I almost grabbed the bucket for myself. Times like these, I think the whole sleepover thing is highly overrated! Whatever happened to making play dates and then going home?

Needless to say, it was a very long night. It did not end there. After throwing both girls into the tub and cleaning up the mess, and disinfecting everything twice, and using up an entire can of Lysol, I heard my daughter loudly whining and tripping to get out of the tub. It seemed her friend was not quite through vomiting. Now, she was crying for her mother and my daughter was begging me to take her home. So I did what any good mother would do. I sprayed some more Lysol and called her mother, waking up their family at a now grueling 3:00 a.m. We agreed to meet somewhere, so I cleaned up the girls and headed off to meet her with bucket and washcloth in hand. When we arrived at the parking lot, her friend had to once more regurgitate. And then we headed home.

I noticed a truck full of cowboys entering the highway and my first thought was that they were from my hometown and they were drunk. I only wish I had been wrong. They slowed quite a bit so I was not too terribly concerned at first. It was not long, however until we hit a construction zone (miles and miles of construction zone) with high barricades and no shoulder. They began to get closer and started veering out of their lane, until they rammed their truck into the cement barricade and swerved across the two lanes. At this point I was officially "freaking out." Then they sped up and were gaining on me. I said a quick prayer asking for an immediate exit and gassed it. God answered my prayer and I was soon on my way home on the feeder road. Just as I had suspected, the drunk cowboys exited Main Street in my hometown and stopped at the corner store.

I forgot to mention that when I got in my car, I realized it was on empty and had to find a gas station open at 3:30 a.m. Just so happens, I had to stop at the gas station with the drunk cowboys. I believe they call that "MURPHY'S LAW". I hate Murphy.

So, when we finally made it home, all I wanted to do was go straight to bed. My daughter crawled into bed with us, so she was one obstacle to my getting any sleep. The other was my constant fear of getting thrown up on. All in all, the night stunk, which led me to today when we were all too tired to go to church this morning.

So, this is proof that life goes on no matter how I feel and what I'm going through. And I should take some solace in the fact that I now have new things to write about in my journal besides just whining about the pain that won't go, go away. ☺

16

Where is My Song?

September 8

Hello again. I've had a horribly depressing weekend and now week. These thoughts and memories come in like a flood and control my mind at times. It's as if nothing I do can take my mind off the situation. I have told my husband that I am sorry for bringing her back into our lives with my thoughts. But I didn't exactly ask for this, nor did I bring her into our lives in the first place. This is all a little more than I can bear at times. Like yesterday -- my five-year old was telling me who she wanted to invite to her birthday party, and she mentioned this woman's two children. Well, I was not expecting that at all, which immediately threw me into a whole slew of memories. I just figured she would have forgotten about them already. They were new and we visited with them only on a few occasions. I guess that was just too much to hope for.

"Please God, help my daughter forget about them. And help me to forget as well."

It's amazing how one day you feel as though everything is okay and then...BAM! It feels like it happened yesterday! How long does this last? When will it fade?

Two of my friends expressed concern for me today. One e-mailed me and said she was worried about me. Another one talked to my mom on the phone and said I wasn't the same. Yes, I'm depressed. And no, I'm not the same. Everything has changed. My outlook on life is different. I am different!

I was just reminded of a testimony I gave in church the last time I sang. Before I sang, "Wonderful, Merciful, Savior", I testified about all that I had gone through and how God was always there giving me strength and hope. How he healed me and loved me through the most difficult times. Why would I think He didn't care after all He's done to show me that He does? About a week before I found out, I sang, "His Eye Is On The Sparrow" at our old church.

I sing because I'm happy/
I sing because I'm free/
His eye is on the sparrow/
And I know He watches me/
Why should I feel discouraged/
Why do the shadows come/
Why does my heart feel lonely/
And long for heaven and home/
When Jesus is my portion/
A constant friend is He/
His eye is on the Sparrow/
And I know He watches me [1]

I do so desperately want to sing again. I just don't have enough energy to sing. Like I'm just too tired. Will I ever sing again? Will I ever believe in fairy tales and love stories and people again?

I was so innocent, trusting and optimistic. Now I feel like I am none of those things anymore.

Sometimes, I want to call her and get some things off my chest. Would it really change anything? Would it make a difference? Would it even make me feel better? I doubt it. I don't want to talk to her. I don't think I actually want to see her face either. Its bad enough I have to see her in my thoughts and dreams. Much worse, if I have to see her in person, I bet. Tramp. How does she live with herself? No conscious, I guess. Her poor kids; I feel sorry for them.

I'm tired and I'm tired of talking about her. She makes me sick. The whole thing does. I will TRY to go to sleep now. Wish me luck. Or better yet, say a prayer for me.

17

Little Reminders

September 17

I am surrounded by little reminders (some bigger than others). And no matter how hard I try to start over fresh and new and "evict" the old life, daily I am still reminded. When will it end? Must this torture continue until the day I die? It seems that way. I thought time with God was supposed to heal all wounds. Has not enough time passed? Or maybe I don't have enough God? Which is it? Both? Please help me Lord. It's killing me.

Earlier today, I was doing great. I was focused on the good that is coming from this. I even e-mailed a friend of mine today asking her to please not be angry at my husband and explaining the wonderful change we are experiencing in our life together. And then something happened. The television happened. I'm beginning to believe all those old codgers who think TV is of the devil. Perhaps they are not as senile as I thought. The shows joke around and make light of affairs. And that's just the sit-coms. The dramas are even worse, because everyone in a drama is having an affair. Or has had one or is about to have one. I don't find that funny at all! And don't even get me started on soap operas. Even if I wanted to, I could never watch one of those again. And is Lifetime really television for women? How about *torture* for women. If I have to sit through another Lifetime movie, I will scream! Why do women do that to themselves? It's depressing!! Who needs to be reminded that their husband cheated on them with a slutty tramp? I sure don't!!! So screw you, TV! You can take your melodramatic, real-life movies and cram them up your antenna for all I care! Viva la Radio!!

18

Kemah & A Wandering Mind

September 20

Just four more days until my daughter's birthday. She will be six years old. We took her to Kemah Saturday for her present (and party) from us. I just couldn't do the whole party thing. There were only a few I actually wanted to invite anyway. And my list and my daughter's list were nowhere near the same. So we took her somewhere. To Kemah. It's no Disneyworld, but it was fun. Fun and HOT! It was like 100° outside. We all smelled great on the way home!! (Sarcasm again) She had a good time and that's all that matters.

It was nice being together on a trip as a family with just me, my husband, and our daughters. We'll have a cookie for her with her grandparents, aunts, uncles, and cousins. So at least she'll get gifts from family. It's not a party with lots of presents but she doesn't really need anything anyway. We'll see how this weekend goes. I feel so unprepared. I hope she can forgive me for not making a huge deal out of her birthday this year like I usually do. This will be the first party that I didn't have over 50 people at. She's used to big blow-out birthday bashes. And this year she's not even having a party. Hopefully we can make up for it. This is just really bad timing...

Oh no. Not again. My mind began to wander. To no other place but, guess where? I'll give you one guess and I bet you get it right on the first try. The sole reason for this entire journal!

I'm enjoying writing, though. Perhaps when this one fills up, I will buy another one. It has been quite helpful. It really helps to get things out and off my chest. This is good for me. Usually I just bottle things up. Apparently, that is not the correct way to deal with this type of situation. Wow. Counseling sure is coming in handy. I may actually learn something from all of this! Perhaps that is exactly what God is hoping for. I heard once that if you don't learn something the first time, then you have to go through it again...

"Please help me learn WHATEVER it is that I'm supposed to learn. I do NOT want to go through this again. My heart will fail me if I do.
Thank you."

19

A Prayer for Healing and Peace

October 1

O.K. First things first…

"Dear Lord,
     Please help my baby sleep straight through the night all night. She finally fell asleep. She has been so sick and unable to rest for a couple of weeks now. Please help her sleep well tonight. Thank you. I also wanted to thank you for us finally hearing back from the district office letting us know the national office approved of us going through the restoration process. I'm so excited. I'm very happy that you want us to continue in the ministry...after we heal, of course. Then I had a nice conversation with the worship leader at our church who seemed excited about me joining the choir. All very good things. It just seems like whenever anything good is trying to happen in our lives, something bad comes. This must be spiritual warfare. You want to bless and heal us and the devil wants to destroy and kill us. I have had just about enough. I HAVE had enough. Please

change this situation. I give it to you, oh Lord. I can't take it anymore. Please do what you do best—miracles! Thank you. There is so much more but I can hardly keep my eyes open. Please protect my daughter while she is away tonight and please help President Bush wins this election. Please bless us financially in a big way for the stress of it all is almost too much to bear. Please heal my family from this sickness. And please continue to heal our marriage. Please help Sunday go well, as we will have a special service with many guests. And give us wisdom, I pray; for wisdom is far more valuable than gold. Thank you. I love you. Goodnight."

20

Anti-Depressants & A Warning Label

November 28

Wow. It's been a while since I've written in here. I suppose one might think I was getting better. I guess in the whole scheme of things, I am considerably better. I have noticed a pattern though. Every month when my hormones are raging, I fall into a deep depression that is very difficult to shake. Perhaps it is the extreme emotional state one suffers during the cycle. Whatever it is, I can almost set a clock to it. I get terribly moody and equally depressed. The counselor has recommended an over-the-counter anti-depressant for times like these.

All things considered, I am doing well and do not need any permanent medication. Only an occasional dose as needed. And that's only should I decide to actually purchase it. We'll see. Besides, Christmas is around the corner and I really need to save my money for all the Christmas gifts I wish to buy instead of medications that I'm a little leery of taking. It's not that I think it will harm me, it's that it comes with a stigma and a small fear or two that a.) someone will find out and think I'm crazy, or b.) I will become addicted, or c.) people will like me better in a drug-induced state as opposed to á la natural! I know. I'm weird. What a burden to have to incessantly worry about such trivial little things.

Today, my husband and I fasted. Mostly for our finances, God's will, and of course, wisdom. I am very much ready to have a place of my own. I just hope that I'm not too discouraged that it is not the nice new home we had before. I did enjoy living there. Although you could not pay me enough now to move back into it. It has been tarnished by the memory of it all. Thankfully, none of our friends live near there, so we should have no reason to ever drive by it. However, as I have so painfully become aware, there is no distance far enough to remove the pain from your memory. There must be a novel on that somewhere. If not, I think I shall write one. It will probably need a warning label, however. One that reads…

WARNING: This novel is extremely depressing and sad. May cause you to try something drastic such as excessive drunkenness, flirtation with a narcotic or bitter revenge.

I don't know why I wrote that. I have no desire to get drunk or smoke dope. I can't say I don't want revenge though. That would be a lie. Well, maybe not completely. At this moment, I don't. I haven't really wanted revenge on my husband. Just her. And I don't necessarily need to inflict this revenge. I just need to know she reaped what she sowed. That tramp. I need forgiveness in my life. Lord knows I've received enough for myself. I need to learn to give it as well. I'm tired.

21

Loneliness & Anticipation

January 13

Here I am again. So much has happened. We rented a house. It seemed like the best deal. Now I spend my days trying to set up house. So many boxes. But I'm slowly making progress. I also miss my parents. I find myself hoping they will stop by, so I won't be so lonely during the day. I went from never having any alone time to having nothing but alone time. Well, as alone as you can get with an 11-month-old baby and a 6-year-old. My oldest did start school here last week, so during the day, it's just me and my baby. My husband tries to come by for lunch when he can. It's very sweet. So much has changed in the last eight months. He is enjoying being with us -- his family -- now. He seems genuinely happy. Something I've never really seen before. And he's much more attentive now. If I need him, I can just tell him now and he doesn't even get mad. He actually tries to help me feel better. I know it must be hard for him to hear me keep bringing it up and dealing with all my new insecurities that didn't exist before. But it's all very overwhelming and quite difficult for me to deal with as well.

    I actually had to take a pregnancy test the other day. It was negative. But I was concerned. My husband says he wants to have another baby with me. I have always wanted three children, so you would think this would make me happy. I just get nervous because I know he didn't even find me remotely attractive while I was pregnant and I can't handle that or any other form of rejection again. So if I do end up pregnant in the very near future, it will not be because we planned it. Besides we really need to pay some bills off before we add to our family again. Maybe by then I can get rid of some of these fears and insecurities. It's not going to happen while I am on my period, though. This is the worst time for the memories to come flooding back. I get depressed and reminded all over again. I'm so sick of the memories. They are still so vivid and I keep re-living the whole horrible ordeal over and over again. Will they ever fade?!

"Please God, help the memories fade and help me to heal!!!"

    I wish His peace would come in like a flood instead of these stupid memories. This year is flying by. I can't believe my baby is almost one year old now. She has grown so quickly. I am NOT looking forward to the holidays that come with the months ahead. I hope I can heal some more before I have to face them. This may be wrong of me, but I think the true test of my husband's change will be how he "handles" these holidays. I'm interested to see what he has planned. Since I've had the absolute worst Mother's Day ever, it shouldn't be too hard to improve upon. Anything remotely nice will be tons better than last year. So, we'll see!

22

On My Knees

February 20

Where to begin...well, for starters, Wednesday night at choir rehearsal, we didn't even get to practice. We usually have about 15 minutes of worship or so before we begin practice. Well, the Spirit fell in that place and I couldn't quit crying. It was awesome and so sweet. Everybody began sharing what the Lord was speaking to them and it was great. Then I felt like God was speaking to me about my identity in Him. I can either be Tara -- the heart broken, bitter, unforgiving, hurt, scorned & betrayed wife. OR I can find who I am in Christ. I am Tara -- child of God, forgiving because I've been forgiven, loved, precious, and an overcoming Godly lady. The latter sounds so much better, don't you think?

I was so much more before all this happened. I had a testimony and personality. I had love and character. Do I really want to allow two people to take that all away from me? I have the opportunity to be all that and more. And if I can get through this victoriously, then I can add so much to my "resume." If I do get through this, I will definitely count that as a victory. Some days are harder than others, but you already know that. Another thing I felt like God was saying was that He wanted me to abandon the pain and hurt and just worship Him. If I could just leave all that hurt and pain in His presence, then He could take it and replace it with healing and forgiveness. So we had a very good time with the Lord and I cried all my makeup off.

Then today when we went to church, Pastor didn't even get to preach. The Spirit fell during worship and it was awesome! I was so free. I was singing along worshiping and singing in the spirit and ad-libbing to the worship and I didn't even worry about what anybody thought. It was great. Then I had this overwhelming desire to fall on my knees. At first I was scared because I was on the platform and I knew everyone would see. Finally, I just couldn't stand up any longer in that strong presence of the Lord, and I fell to my knees weeping uncontrollably. The tears were pouring out faster than I could wipe them away. At some point right before that I had been praying that God would help me to forgive so that it wouldn't eat me alive and consume me. I prayed I could forgive just as He forgave…me and them. I not only *wanted* to forgive, but I NEEDED to forgive so that I could be free. The only person I was hurting was me and I was sick of it.

We met a great new couple Saturday night and I almost didn't give myself a chance to find out because initially I could not get over her uncanny resemblance to that other woman. All I kept thinking was, "Very funny, God. You must really want me to forgive her, huh?"

Anyway, as the worship progressed, I began praying for God to take away the pain. The PAIN that goes way down deep, deep, deep in my being. The PAIN that makes me want to throw up if I think on it too long. The PAIN that always makes me cry anytime I think about it. I prayed He would go way down and jerk it out by its very root. It was about that time that I found myself on my knees weeping before the Lord.

Eventually I looked up a bit to find more than half the church was also on their knees bowing before the Lord. Some were even laid out on their faces before God. Soon, the music pastor couldn't even play the keyboard and sing anymore, so some of the musicians just began to play quietly. Then the spirit fell on the congregation. It was so awesome, because no one told everyone to get on their knees and no one told everyone to pray. It just sort of happened and was completely God-led. This went on so long that we didn't have a sermon and we got out after one o'clock. But the cool thing was that it didn't even feel that late. I wasn't even hungry. I think I could have stayed there forever.

But it did end and my contacts were so cloudy from all the tears that I couldn't see a thing. Everything was blurry, and it was okay. Usually if I have a good cry, I inevitably get a crying headache, but not today. Isn't that neat? I just knew that God did a work and a healing in me and I can't wait to reap the benefits!! There is so much more I want to write about but just writing about today has reminded me of how thoroughly exhausted I am. So I'll be back soon.

"Thank you God for everything! I love you and I am ready for a change!"

23

Setbacks & Jerks

March 15

Last night I had a meltdown. It was so weird because it's been a while since I've had one. And it's really amazing how something so seemingly small can set me off like that. My husband made one joking comment and that was it for me. And he didn't even mean anything by it. But immediately my mind started racing.

It triggered thoughts of me being fat and totally self-conscious. A lump rose up in my throat and I was fighting back tears. I couldn't breathe and then I couldn't fight anymore. Just when I was starting to feel better about everything -- another setback.

Today I found out that a lady I know is getting a divorce and is completely devastated. Her husband had an affair and she wanted to try to work things out but he didn't. He chose the other woman over her and left his wife. Almost 20 years of marriage and it gets tossed aside for what? I'm just glad my husband wanted to stay with me.

This guy I know has been flirting with me for a while. Little winks here and there. Smiles followed by gazes that last a little too long. So, is this how it began? I know that I hold the power to encourage this behavior or end it. Kind of scary. On the one hand, I am flattered. On the other, I know the devastating end result if this kind of behavior is left to continue. In my efforts to not hurt his feelings, I suppose I have not been clear enough. But, I think maybe he is finally getting the hint that I am not interested. Guys like that really make me angry. And then when I think about his wife being pregnant, it infuriates me.

Men can be so frustrating sometimes. If they spent half as much time nurturing the relationships they already have as they do lusting after other men's wives, then we might all have some pretty descent relationships. But no, they have to think with their lower extremities most of the time and be jerks. I need to stop and pray before I talk myself into hating all men. Oh, help me Lord.

24

Life Lessons

April 6

Things I've learned in life…(and it wasn't in kindergarten!)

Lesson #1: Life's bird is going to eventually "dump" on your head. So, wash your hair or stink while you whine!

Lesson #2: Watch what you say! The only thing worse than fighting, is having to apologize afterward.

Lesson #3: (Thankfully I did not have to learn this one through personal experience!) The grass is NOT greener on the other side. All grass has weeds and all rose bushes have thorns!

---

1. Martin, Civilla D. and Gabriel, Charles H. "His Eye is On the Sparrow." Lyrics. Gospel Hymn. 1905.

25

The Anniversary

Mother's Day

I am sitting on the beach listening to the calming sound of the waves clapping onto the shore, with the wind caressing my face. My six-year old is creating a masterpiece in the sand while my husband walks along the shore with my 15-month-old hand in hand. It's like a postcard, only better. In postcards, they take the most amazing pictures that you can't even believe exist, and place them on the front. This moment, if captured by photography, would be my favorite postcard. But this surreal moment and all the peaceful emotions cannot be captured by a picture. And that's what makes it even better than a postcard.

It's hard to believe it's been one whole year since my world came crashing down around me and sent me spiraling into a devastating abyss of hurt, pain, and loneliness. But at this very moment, I am okay. The week leading up to this day left me in question of whether or not I would recover. The anticipation and anxiety have left my head reeling with doubts and fears.

Combine that with the ever-interesting series of nightmares that have been faithfully coming to me every night, and you have a pretty stressful and aggravating week. Plus, my baby decided to cut five new teeth this week. Lack of sleep, haunting nightmares when I do sleep, extreme insecurity, and constant fear make for a sure-fire, fun-filled holiday!!

I'm not sure what I thought would happen, but I am sure that this peaceful day on the beach is not at all what I expected.

"Thank you God. Thank you for protecting me and loving me and caring for me."

I woke up to the gentle touch of a loving husband tickling my thigh. And when I opened my eyes, I was greeted by the warmest smile full of love. And an endearing look I have grown to love and adore!

26

The Diary of a Mad White Irish Girl

September 12

  I just finished watching, "Diary of a Mad Black Woman," by Tyler Perry. I laughed. I cried. It moved me. I know it was the diary of a mad black woman, but it could have been excerpts from my own diary. Some of the entries were dangerously close to being identical to some of my own. Ironic.

  I know it seems I've stopped writing. I guess I have, in a way. Some time ago God gave me a love and passion for His word again. So I've been reading it, and enjoying every minute of it. I have a separate notebook that I've been writing down all the scriptures that have just popped out at me from right off the page. I love how it has come alive to me.

  Sunday morning, I am singing a special in church. It's

"We Speak to Nations." It's for a missions' conference we're starting Sunday. I LOVE how God has put a song in my heart again. I wondered if I would ever sing again. Not just sing, but sing with passion, conviction, and with every fiber within me. And He did. I don't know when the exact moment was, but I am oh so thankful that it finally came.

> *"Flowers appear on the earth, the season of singing has come."* (Song of Solomon 2:12)

I guess I need a new journal. I've seen the next page, which also happens to be the last page and I can't think of a better way to end this journal. It's a doodle from my daughter who wanted to leave a little note for me telling me that she loves me, not knowing how important this book was to me. But I did not get mad. Because her "doodle" just raised the value of this book for me, and I can't help but smile when I see the treasure.

27

By the Grace of God

Three years after the matter...

Guess what? Still breathing. It's been 3 years, 2 months, and 10 days since my world came crashing in on that fateful day. I am very happy to say that I can breathe without thinking, I got my song back and I must admit that it didn't kill me. It actually made me stronger. I can honestly say that I am thankful for it. While I would never want to go through it again, I am thankful. God turned all the bad around for good. He brought healing to me and my husband. He gave forgiveness and mercy and grace.

He also gave us another baby and a fresh start on a new life together. I have the husband and marriage that I have always wanted and I didn't even have to get a divorce to find it. Through counseling, we learned to communicate openly and honestly with each other. We are so very close now. Our relationship is relaxed and actually fun. We have been bound together by a new covenant.

A very wise man told us in the beginning that time with God heals all wounds. He was right. Time with God did heal our wounds. Sure, there's a scar. But only to remind me of how far God has brought us. And for that, I am truly grateful.

Forgive and forget. I have felt the redemptive power of God's forgiveness flow from my very own heart. And I have forgotten many of the small details. But mostly my bad memories have been replaced with good ones of how God rescued me out of the pit, walking with me every step of the way, and carrying me when I needed it. Restoring me the only way He knows how… perfectly.

"Thank you God for healing and grace. You have kept all your promises. You have been faithful to deliver me and have taught me to trust again. In you alone I place my trust. Thank you for not only repairing my marriage, but making it better than I expected. Thank you for teaching me your ways, like forgiveness, for they truly are higher than our own. Thank you for being my strength, strong tower, and refuge. For always being the Great I Am. You are My Everything."

"He hath made everything beautiful in His time…"
Ecclesiastes 3:11, KJV

Epilogue

Today

There is a scripture in the bible that talks about cleaning house and if you are not careful, the enemy will return seven times stronger. (Luke 11:24-26) The enemy will try to test your decision to walk out your healing to see if it is true. And if you open the door again, you give him authority to come in seven times stronger than before. This is truth and reality. There was a Round 2 for us and our marriage, but sometimes the enemy doesn't know who he is dealing with.

After completely healing from the infidelity, my faith in God grew stronger. The worse the pain, the greater the gain. My faith in God grew and grew and grew. I gained the realization that My God was the same God yesterday, today, and forever, (Hebrews 13:8). All the Bible stories I had learned in Sunday School took on new meaning. They weren't just good stories about some people a long time ago. They were examples of His awesome power and strength. A testimony of His grace and mercy. A triumphant wave of redemption and freedom. They were examples of what He could do for ME. He hasn't changed. He doesn't lose power over time. He did it before. He can do it again. It is possible to go through the fire and come out not singed and without even the smell of smoke on you (Daniel 3:27). The more trials that came, the deeper my worship to God became.

When the enemy came back in, he came like a flood. We didn't understand the importance of putting on the full armor of God so that you are able to withstand the enemy, (Ephesians 6:11). Recently, the Lord gave me a vision of His army. We were all standing around talking and visiting. Our armor was scattered around us on the ground. Some of us had several pieces on, but missing others. I had most of my armor on, but I was leaning on my shield. It was like we were all taking a break. The enemy walked right up in the midst of us and no one even noticed. He barely pushed me on my shoulder and I stumbled backwards. Then, I realized who it was. I scrambled around to pick up my shield and the sword and told him to hold on. Of course, he didn't. He pushed me again; this time knocking me to the ground. After that, God came in and showed me His army again and what we needed to be. The entire army was completely covered in armor and linked together in rows and columns. Strong, vigilant, watchful, and ready. I knew that I had let my guard down.

So, when the enemy came in again, as we should have expected, we weren't prepared. Round 2 did not lessen the impact of my healing chronicled in this book, but it did shake my faith in if I could do it again. My husband was getting weakened by the repeated temptations of the enemy and he made some really bad choices. While there was no physical affair again, our relationship had been compromised. I wasn't sure I had the strength to go through the healing process again or if I even wanted to. We took a trip to Dallas for ministry from a wonderful couple, BJ and Donna Compton, who were trained by Restoring The Foundations for individual and couples ministry.

We learned that there are many ways the enemy can come in. It is the reason that you can seemingly overcome something, only to deal with it again later on down the road. We needed complete healing and deliverance. And that is just what we got. God used this ministry to free us from generational curses, ungodly beliefs, soul and spirit hurts, and demonic oppression. The biggest thing for us was to reject all of the ungodly beliefs that we had accepted as truth through previous hurts and word curses spoken over us. God revealed to us new Godly beliefs to replace the ungodly ones. God also gave us new identity statements. He spoke to us very clearly about who we are in Him. What God thinks about us. What His Word says about us. As we began to accept His Word and these new Godly beliefs, our hearts began to change toward each other. We saw each other through God's eyes. There was an acceleration in our healing and forgiveness and we now walk daily together in the strength of our Lord.

    I'm Still Standing! You can too!

    Your Friend,
    Tara Vincent

"Be prepared. You're up against far more than you can handle on your own. Take all the help you can get, every weapon God has issued, so that when it's all over but the shouting you'll still be on your feet. Truth, righteousness, peace, faith, and salvation are more than words. Learn how to apply them. You'll need them throughout your life. God's Word is an indispensable weapon. In the same way, prayer is essential in this ongoing warfare. Pray hard and long. Pray for your brothers and sisters. Keep your eyes open. Keep each other's spirits up so that no one falls behind or drops out,"
(Ephesians 6:13-18, The Message).

www.ingramcontent.com/pod-product-compliance
Lightning Source LLC
Chambersburg PA
CBHW071327040426
42444CB00009B/2100